AMERICAN RAPTURE

Poems from a Heartscape

Jordan Claire McCraw

Imperfection Press

Printed in the United States of America

First Printing, 2020

ISBN 978-1-7353356-0-5

Library of Congress Control Number: 2020912391

Imperfection Press

www.imperfectionpress.com
www.jcmccraw.com

Photographs by Jimmy Fontaine

For my son, Julian
Who created me

For my husband, Tom
Who carried me through it

I realized that love can be mediocre and a safe comfort, or it can be unhinged and hurtful. Either seemed like a good life.

-Terese Marie Mailhot, *Heart Berries*

Contents

AMERICAN RAPTURE

Poems from a Heartscape

American Rapture

Jordan Claire McCraw

I come from a long tradition of
Blue-collar heartbreak
We assault our fields with a shovel
And then beat our wives to bed
The romance practically writes itself

American rapture

You say i would break you
You matter, so much
But a part of me whispers
I would be your lucky day

I matter, too

It's... unavoidable
People will ask
Where is your mother
I say she died
If they ask how
I say she left

They don't ask why

If we were back on the high line
I would call out and ask you to stop
I would put my hand in your pocket

It was cold

Jordan Claire McCraw

When my pieces come together
If they can
Will we still fit

Because you broke this

When the only voice that mattered
The one i heard in the womb
The high-pitched laugh that bent her in two
When that voice said *they will leave you*
When they know who you are
They will leave you
Every one

It rendered all else worthless
All the kind words
All the affirmations
Across countries
Across continents
So many compliments

They will leave you
When they know who you are
They will leave you

So i lie in wait with a shotgun
Your love is my cue to get down
I pull a cap down to my eyes
This camo pattern jacket
You will leave
I will fight you, motherfucker
I am ready

Now you know

Jordan Claire McCraw

You left

Thank you for kissing my scar

My lips mean nothing

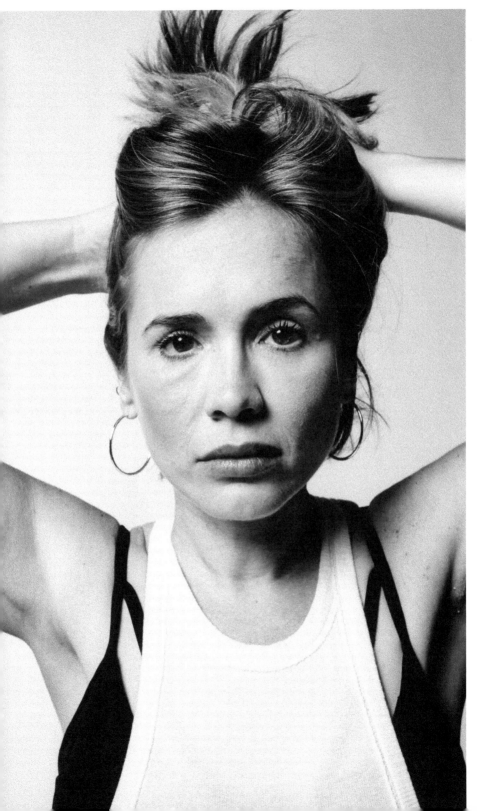

My son won't stop talking
He's got so much to say
But i am still here
I have things to say

A mother

Jordan Claire McCraw

If wounds can close
And scars can fade
As i heal with new dimensions
And you are not here
To claim your seat
Will you not stay in play
Will you be unwritten
Will there be no place left for you
In me

Head count

What the fuck is the plot of
Paw patrol

A mother, pt 2

Maybe now she is free
To present not as whole
But in pieces

Rebirth announcement

Moments like this, it's like
...you brought me back
I want to make something to hold
To a lamp
I want to project snowflake patterns
On walls
To admire them all night long

First flush

Jordan Claire McCraw

I opened some random newspaper
On a cold, wet autumn evening
And i smelled an english morning

My other home

American Rapture

Does missing you cause cancer

Fucked

Why is that girl, her neck so long from looking over
Fences, allowed to walk around here
Looking dead? hold her and never let go

The easy answer

Some nights
I still can't look at other men
So i sleep in your shirt
And i pretend you joined the army

Tour of duty

Jordan Claire McCraw

You are the only
Person i know
Who can hurt me like this
I will run at you stumbling
I will say sorry first
Please, what can i do

I want to fix it

I hear he killed himself
During peak commuter hours
In my other country's time zone
In some very public way

Six months later

I am convinced
That if i had money
I would want myself

Turned off

You say i am all *me/ me/ me*
But i ask you, how else
Should i apologise
Over and over
For everything

First person

I'm lucky to even still be here
I come with care instructions
I require maintenance
Or i will break

Artifact

Being a mother
Is the best thing
That ever happened to me

It is now my life's work

To reconcile
My best thing
Being too much for me

Postpartum

I remember
When i couldn't breathe
In the good way

When i posted

Some dumb photo

Of me smiling

In my new clothes

That i knew you'd like

If you were a girl

I'd imagined her

When i chose them

Notifications

Jordan Claire McCraw

I remember
When you messaged me
Are you free to talk

And then i knew

I knew in that moment
That i would get hurt
Yeah sure, i'm free

It might not happen

Black holes are made
When a man and a woman
Are in love but refuse
To admit it; while trying
To circumvent physics
They drown

Impassable

So i don't know how
To say this

I just don't know how
To bring it up

But i feel like
You should know

That when

You told me you loved me
While you were touching me
But it turned out
You didn't mean it

My body

It became less special

And now i have to live in it

The silly little housewife
Once she had it all in spades
And she could finally relax
Was just so paralysed with boredom
Uninspired, numb and lacking
That she caused herself some pain
Pawned her heart so you could break it
Just to see how she would take it
Just to watch herself react

The hobbyist

Jordan Claire McCraw

My therapist stares at me
How do you feel

I don't look away
Like a house that burned down

Arsonist

You're saying something
Kind words
I just can't listen

You're looking at me
Kind eyes
I just can't look up

I'm just so sorry
I can't
His ghost's behind you

Letting go

Jordan Claire McCraw

Go look after your son, you say
You, who i was brave enough to call
In my lowest moment

Get off the phone and be present
But i called because you know me
I'm a good mom
And my baby boy, he's perfect
Say we'll make it
Say you're sorry that he kicked me

Tell me things like this just happen

Friend with no kids

Every time i close my eyes
I hear a polaroid flapping

No image materialises

I know that we've stopped making memories

Overexposure

Jordan Claire McCraw

I can't sleep at all
I wander to your pillow

I shovel in and breathe
I kiss your doughy fists
And stroke your downy head

Do you know that i'm still here
Can you feel me holding you

Do you know that i'll come back from this

Back to you

Outperforming
Your bullshit
Is exhausting

Why do i
Have to squeeze
Between your cracks
To fucking sleep at night

I'm done with you

Jordan Claire McCraw

I dream of passing you on sidewalks
I fall asleep and dream
Of passing you on sidewalks

Ghost

"It has long since come to my attention that people of accomplishment rarely sat back and let things happen to them. They went out and happened to things."

-Leonardo da Vinci

It has also been said that
Love is all that binds
The universe

I bind you together
With my exquisite love
I am accomplished in
My happening to you

Sit back

After all this
Time. i see your face

I decide to
Breathe. in and out

The choice

Jordan Claire McCraw

If i starve myself
To be beautiful for you
Will you hunger for me

Will the hunger keep you up at night
Will you panic to suck on my elbow
Or nibble my collarbone

If i waste away in your arms
Will i become the perfect burden
Will my eyes look wide as saucers

Forgotten wife

Knowing you are all mine
Is no fun at all

I want to fight for you
Two or three more times

Other half

I reach for the dental floss
In the medicine cabinet

I close the cabinet door
You quirk one eyebrow

When did you become
A reflection in my mirror

Why do i still end my days
With you

Get out

Jordan Claire McCraw

You stuff me in a burlap sack
With other bastard pups

As you toss me from the riverbank
I fear you'll be alone

My darling, i'll wait for you, i cry
I promise not to die

One promise kept

I would feel so glamorous
Sitting alone
In this café

If i had come with a plan
Instead of fucked
With a journal

Tuesday, central park

The ancient egypt exhibit
Can suck my dick
With the bench where you sat
Outside of it

Dead friend

Never say sorry
To a fucking guy
For my postpartum tits

Tits should have a story
What is his story

Stronger sex

Jordan Claire McCraw

You never painted me
Before you packed your things

Will the world remember
My breasts as you saw them

Impressionist

A quick-fingered sun
Licks homes under bridges
To the birdsong of
Rear parking sensors
Until crates are dropped

Manhattan, first morning

Jordan Claire McCraw

My son arrested me
With his toy handcuffs

Now he can't find the key

I really want a snack

Fuck a duck

Dutifully, i
Eat you until i feel numb
Which is quite like full

Boring salad haiku

Jordan Claire McCraw

I stopped manifesting
In a foreign public sector

I got on well, though
Only called my labor union twice

If being invisible
Meant the same thing everywhere, i
Could explain it to y'all

Assimilated

When i hear a song, i panic

I turn you off

You are every song

I miss music

Jordan Claire McCraw

God grant me
The serenity
To accept this man will not change his mind
The courage
To love myself without his arms around me
The wisdom
To know his opinion never meant shit

Pit stop chapel

It is difficult
To see my worth
With short hair
Because i guess
I have less of it

Casting call

Jordan Claire McCraw

I'd laugh with the windows down
I'd keep water bottles in the trunk of my car
I'd have year-round nose freckles
I'd give boys the finger at red lights
I'd feel neon pink on the inside
I'd be a baseball fan because, ya know, my dad

California girl back-up plan

Google postpartum psychosis
When you google baby blues

Google episiotomy recovery
When you google natural birth

Google dysphoric milk ejection reflex
When you google nipple creams

Do women a favor

Jordan Claire McCraw

I keep entangling my worth
In my disappointing outcomes

Not a failure

My therapist asked me
This week
Can you notice your triggers

I notice you
When i see my body naked
And it is alone

I tell the therapist
I have been triggered
By food

Maslow's hierarchy

If i never got to be sixteen
Is it too late for me
To sit in my car drinking cheap beer
With bad boys

Would i even enjoy fucking up
Would it even give me closure

Sixteen years later

My body wasn't meant to waste away
In a parlor
By a window
With sunlight on brandy
Or second-hand smoke

My people didn't know your people

My body is built to haul tubers from dirt
To can butter beans
Tighten mason jar lids
Wipe my long, bony fingers
On muslin

I sweat on my belly

Two generations later/ cattle call

Good morning

I see it is sunny

I will make toast

I will then eat it

With my clothes on

Positive self-talk

So many clean towels
I could wear them all day
And shuffle to the fridge for chocolate pudding
When i wanted it

Shuffle shuffle

Psych ward fo eva

Jordan Claire McCraw

Is the destination
Hollywood

Or getting home safely
To my kid

Made it

I used to miss you
All the time

Now it's only when
I panic

Learned association

Jordan Claire McCraw

A tragedy, to medicate
The artist

To moderate her fits
Of passion

You may stabilize
Her vitals

You may keep the bitch
Alive

Grounded flight

You are brilliant

But when that mortal
Looked straight
At the sun
He went blind

Not your fault

Jordan Claire McCraw

When i arrive strong
And pre-assembled
Tight waist, with a smile
The boys go wild

She's a warrior

But once i tell them
How hard it was
To get here, i'm hungry
And fucking depressed

She talks too much

Better on instagram

When you ask
Who here can do it
My hand goes up
Knowing full well
I will improvise
For attention

Impostor syndrome

I will not
Exile
The parts
Of me
That loved
You

I will
Paint
Them on
My coat
Of
Arms

Everyone
Will know
The hero's
Long
Walk
Ended

Tapestry

Once i am
Real
No longer your
Fantasy
Let's say you
Hurt me
And now i am
Broken
And now i have
Questions

It's so inconvenient
Innit

Pick up your mess

But then
They read her poetry
And realised
They never deserved her
Not for a moment
And not at all

Beautiful inside

You say i've come back to you
No, my beloved
Just look at you

I've come forward

Jordan Claire McCraw

The girls at pre-k
Said to my son
Boys don't wear nail polish

Here we go

Honey, those girls are basic

I don't apologise
For what i said
When i was hungry

#sorrynotsorry

Jordan Claire McCraw

Aww, don't worry
That you're in the back

Nosebleed seats
Are better than nothing

That's what mega screens
Are for

You'll see all the highlights
Baby

Stalking my ass

Look over the railing, my darling
A big storm is coming
Get up on your tippy-toes

First fireflies

Jordan Claire McCraw

It is now
My job
To make sure
He forgets you

You left him

You're not his hero

I knew i would fail
And something would kill us
I mourned you alive

I cried everywhere
Our time was all borrowed
All borrowed, all borrowed

First child

You apologise

I flinch

What's this trick
More smoke and mirrors
Rabbit in a fucking hat

Narcissist

I love your earrings/ watch your tone
Yes, everything is on
The table

If you want my compliments
You suffer my appraisal

Grown-ass woman

Jordan Claire McCraw

And then there was a breeze
In all this space
The curtains flapping

I saw things differently
And not with anger, but with
Sudden, thoughtful questions

Open mind

I keep walking
Past you

Snapping your
Stem

Carrying bags

My grip is
Too loose

I'm leaving your
Roots

In the ground

I can't forget

Jordan Claire McCraw

The dead rat
Would have made you crazy

But people
Have to pick their battles

And no one
Wants to scrape it up

What's left

I made the husband
Start working out

Forever is long

Jordan Claire McCraw

Maybe just this one time
If i can be bothered
I'll meet you at a bar

I might laugh at your jokes
I might not laugh at them
Or we could just make out

Fuck it/ take me

Jordan Claire McCraw

There comes a time
When every woman
Wants to feel her back
Smack against a wall

Take over

My ancestors were
Hot-blooded confederates

Muskets, drink and cigarettes

I'd fight those rascals up and down

A quick-tongued yankee

Jordan Claire McCraw

If you
Want to, like
Lick me

You'll have
To, like
Brush your teeth first

Respect the space

I found my peace
And made new friends
Am so much stronger
          somehow happy

And now, i guess you'll never know
That i became a supermodel

Blocked

If i feel good
You swagger up

To let me know
I'm chicken shit

Why hang around
Inside my head

I can't evict
A poltergeist

The dickhead clause

You were gone
Gone
Gone

I could see it
With my telescope

A fucking constellation

You were gone
You punched the sky

Over and out

I work out
So one day
I'll look good
In sweatpants

#momgoals

If it wasn't
For girlfriends
I think
I would murder
You all

The men in my life

A mother leaves her baby in a basket
In the reeds
It floats away

I am her baby in the basket

Downstream daughter

Jordan Claire McCraw

Three times
This month
I heard him say

My mommy's favorite color
Is the color of my lips

Will those have been
My three best moments

How much longer

It ruined all
The family photos

With your arm
Around my shoulders

And your face
A whipping boy

The silent rage

Jordan Claire McCraw

Read to me
And cup my ass
Leave the paragraph unfinished

Rainy sunday

I breathe you out
I breathe me in
I breathe you out
I breathe me in

On life support

I breathe you out

Until, one day
I breathe me in

I breathe me out

Surviving the discard

It turns out

The only revenge

Against you

For breaking me

Into a million

Bajillion pieces

Is to not care

I'll get right on that

After i put my son to bed

And lift my arms

To wash my hair

Narcissists win battles

Too bad
Though

To know that
You

Will always

Hate yourself

You lose the war

If i was a man
I'd want you full

I'd want to probe
The depth of your dimples

I'd make your belly button talk
To hear you laugh
And lick accordion folds
From breast to navel

I'd want you satisfied
By wine
And then by chocolate cake
And then by me

So eat the food

I still love to run
At the high school track
Smell the sun on polyurethane

I always did the track
Then had a dannon coffee yogurt

If you freeze a coffee yogurt
It will last 10x as long

Happy memories in which i happened to be sick

Jordan Claire McCraw

Dear young hollywood

Breathe
Life
Back
Into
The
Oceans

With all your money

Please

Microplastics

The headline reads
Kylie jenner says
Becoming a mom
Improved her sex life

Bitch becoming a mom
Happened at the same time
That you became
A billionaire

I said it

Jordan Claire McCraw

My baby
Shook with fever
As we ran into the
Pharmacy

I raced him
To the tylenol
And spooned it to him
Instantly

I would have
Stolen that
Or sold my body
If I had to

Why a mommy goes to jail

I would rather buy peaches in winter
I would rather apply for a checkbook

I would rather do almost anything
Than look around and honor the present

You weren't supposed to be a memory
Until i forget you i cannot breathe

Staying busy

Jordan Claire McCraw

I have heard
That everyone
Knows the real you
A little differently

It must be so much work

How many soulmates do you have

Fake news fuckboy

My daddy
Always found it from somewhere

No crisis
He couldn't get us all through

No dresses
Tore up that weren't then replaced

I didn't
Know how he stayed up at night

When money was tight

Jordan Claire McCraw

If i call a psychic from a phone booth

If i tell her my name is jerry

If i just ask, *does anyone miss me*

Can i find out if you miss me

Can i do it without your soul tracking me

My coordinates

People sleeping in their cars
Just watched me kick a concrete pole
And watched me scream
And wail and wipe
The sticky makeup off my samsung

The broken place just let me cry
I threw myself against the wall
It smelled of piss
I sobbed about you
Oh, i gambled and lost

Casino garage

I've longed to dangle
Pale crescent breasts
And pigeon-coo
On fragrant nights
Bewitching boys
In rhododendrons

Juliet's balcony

Jordan Claire McCraw

Thank you for waiting
Until i resurfaced
With sticks in my hair
And said *i tried*
But failed

Unconditional love

The people
Who want to spend
Their only $150
On a hoodie
Are my people

Important shit

I'm shredding zucchini
Swish swish swish

I'm coring some apples
Chop chop chop

I'm singing and smiling
Filling up freezer bags
Prepping for winter

My husband is worried

All
Daddies
Should
Vouch
For
Their
Little
Girls

Thanks, dad

Jordan Claire McCraw

The bravest thing
I can think of

Is to follow my dream
When i know it might fail

And to stick around
For the verdict

Perhaps a public execution

Olympic gold

My son will watch

Character outlasts personality

It is rarely the people i laughed with
Who hold my hand on muddy slopes
Or save my dreams from crocodiles

In my thirties

One of the mothers
Who claimed me
Because the universe
Can be kind
Declared, *there is no*
Testimony
Without a test

My parable

I've scattered the ashes
Of all my remains
On all of your heads
For the umpteenth time

Another audition

I keep meaning
To make a vision board
But then my poetry
Is my vision board

Words
Just
Come
Out
Looking
Like
Colors

Declaring intention

I think in small whispers
And feel in big booms

Is life really that simple

Jordan Claire McCraw

When i smell rot on front porch steps
Or hear the squeak of chipped screen doors
And i see someone running barefoot
My heart just up and activates
I want to climb into a loft
Where pa can't find me

Southern blood

You know what's been
A goddamned nuisance

Rising above
My mother's choices

Still that kid

I'm stuffed in a trenchcoat
On somebody's shoulders
Posed next to adults
Who were born with a chance
And i'm just so exhausted
From sneaking through doors
Out-thinking great-nephews
Out-charming heiresses

A new york impostor

Coffee is a stimulant
My drug of choice
I own that shit
So what's your vice
We all need something

Don't be perfect

Jordan Claire McCraw

It's who i can count on
To listen and nod
When i say i've fucked up

They say, *i get it*

Other mothers

I haven't seen her in twenty years
We're very different in several ways
But we're standing here naked
While sharing a bathroom
And spilling our tea

Just like sisters

Jordan Claire McCraw

Sister
He hurt you
We'll talk about him
He'll pay for his crimes
At the hands of your family

But first
Let's talk about you
With the french doors blown open
Pale curtains fluttering
Orchids in vases
Preparing this home
For such terrible guests

And then letting them stay

Let's heal you first

I talked to god
Last night

By that i mean

I screeched at her

BITCH, HELP ME OUT

Negotiations

I think i love too deeply

All the cool kids
Think i'm weak

I want respect for taking punches

Empath problems

In the teachers' lounge
With kirsty's homemade lemon cake
And workbooks stacked up to my ears
The kettle humming in the corner
Rain is streaming down the windows
Someone's jammed the copier
The knuckles rapping on the door
   Miss/ miss/ miss/ miss...

Where my heart goes on the greyhound

On my way to therapy, i heard
Miss, he waved his lucozade
And ran out into traffic
Thumped my car's boot with his fist
I nearly had a heart attack

Or the time at marks and spencer, when
She rang up all my shopping
Condoms and a first response test
Shitshit, did i teach this girl
I could have blown myself away

When i first moved out of town
I thought, *thank god there's no more spies*
But now i'm safe, i realise
They were my heart

I miss my kids

You gently tug my bra

I turn the other way

I only want to grow
My resumé

Money moves

Jordan Claire McCraw

Mommy, will you bake for me

The oven is preheated
Can of pumpkin on the counter
Something festive
Breathe and stir
Don't lick the bowl

Make sure he sees you smile

Better for my baby

One of my voices, let's call him joe
Starts to hang up bunting
In my head

The other voices scream: *no, joe*

And joe just stands there shamefaced
Up a ladder
No balloons again?

No, joe

He quietly descends

No cakes are baked
And no one breathes
We sit in silence
While you're out to dinner
Somewhere in the world
And feel surrounded
By the people
Who most love you

On your birthday

Jordan Claire McCraw

I started doing stand-up
When I realised that my suffering
Was just so fucking funny
And the toy handcuffs fell off

We laughed and laughed

Primary food
Is what feeds your soul

Secondary food
Goes in your mouth

I guess that's why
England made me fat

Cold, wet and bored

Jordan Claire McCraw

I went to a monastery
To sit and write in peace

I spent most of the afternoon
On social media

Then i picked up and left quickly
So my instagram followers wouldn't find the location and rape me

Meditation

Change the goddamn world

Go tell everyone
How cruel you are
To you

And why you shouldn't be

The feminist

Jordan Claire McCraw

Even now, if i'm in public
And i smell it
I just wilt

Being anybody's princess
Made me skinny dip in daylight

Every word you said was gospel
All the lies just came out roses

Cheap cologne

I have boundaries now
I say no
But at what cost

I just look them in the eye
And say *this doesn't sit with me*

What's the worst that they can do
Not be my friend
Here are my rules
You stay, you play

Or move along

Jordan Claire McCraw

I scratched back out
Completely spooked
I stood there panting

Rosaries and paper cups
Dime store teddy bears face-down

Wet petals découpaged on limestone
So, you'd done it, then
But look at me

I pulled a tree root from my hair
I twisted it between my fingers

Buried alive

You'll wonder if they have more blankets
Pudding cups will taste like pie
You'll suck on ice chips in a cup
Perhaps a nurse will brush your hair

If you wake up

Don't kill yourself

Legs slick with bubbles
I'm just so damn tired

My baby's in bed
I drank all our wine
This bath has gone cold

What are your plans, then
For me once I'm dry

I've long given up
On making this fun
You'll have to be quick

Know i love you

I know now, god
Is watching me
And wreaking havoc
By design
That I'm a storyteller
I must live to tell the tale
So I'll be fine

Put here to talk

Jordan Claire McCraw

I wonder what it's like
To swipe right

I got married before
All of this

Fomo

I think about the forest
How you burned it to the ground
And how i let you

After everything had died
I let you burn it to the ground
I let you think that this was arson

Let you think you'd killed it all
You crazy cowboy
Look at you, you torched a forest

I was fertilised by ash

New ecosystem

Jordan Claire McCraw

Love of my life
You had my womb
And then my youth
You eat my food
Just let me watch
One video
On youtube

Give my phone back

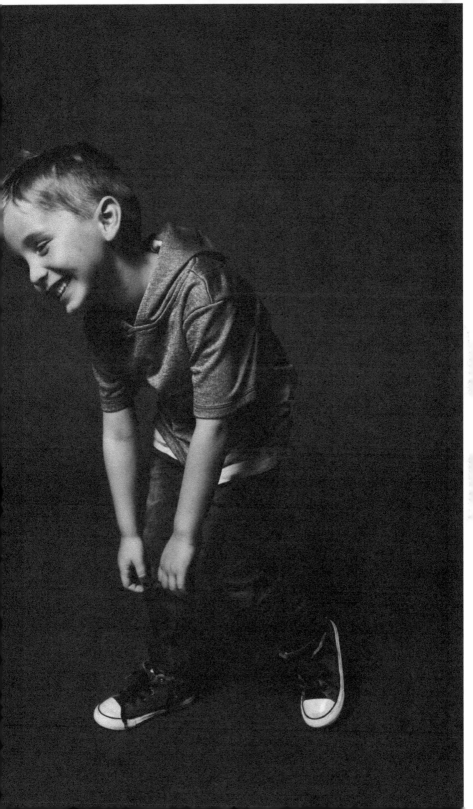

Somebody
Wrote a song
About you

I heard it
Between bites
Of bagel

Traffic on
95
Was crawling

I learned the
Words behind
A dump truck

Morning fm

Jordan Claire McCraw

I do not know how to
Fill in this paperwork

I am two different things
In two very different ways

Bicultural applicant

I pulled up. *are you feeling better*

Oh, you know. just waiting, now
The biopsy

I breathed, *i see*

So this is one of those
Interminable times
You don't know how you'll make it
Then you're out the other side
Facing interminable times

We're all adults here

Jordan Claire McCraw

If these trees could talk
They'd say i used to up and climb them
Fool's gold pirate ships
With epic masts for limbs
And i would stay up there for hours
Using toothpaste on my hands
To scrub off sap

Now i only rake their leaves

I got so boring

If i ask you
For a favor
Know i'm dying
I must love you
I would rather
Face my family
Penniless

No secrets here

When i auction off
My body
Will it ask a higher price
If all the thoughts i have
Are simple
And i don't require xanax
Just to drive a car
Or make myself a sandwich

What a gem

I'm pretty sure
My family
Disapproves
Of all my poems
Wishes i
Would keep my mouth shut
Wonders why
I come here screaming
Phones up when
They think i'll publish

Troublemaker

Passes out of class
If they are feeling out of sorts
So they aren't pressured to conform
While suffering

Thank god we now face *mental health*
But litigation culture blinds
And if these kids don't learn to feel
They're fucking doomed

The british schools

All of them have suffered
They are all confetti cannons
In black holes
Bewitching you
From outer space
What could they do
From right next door

The beauty contest

Play my body
Like your bass guitars

Are you still an atheist

The white boy

When you stuck me like a pig
Spat on the blade
Declared you never loved the beast

You gave me so much inspiration
Since then, i've been damn prolific

Awesome content

There will be moments
When you're not as sick
And you will realise what you did
And i will not be there to hold you
'Cus you fucked this shit right up
And i just wish that i could see it
I could sit there on your desk
And be invisible
Just watch you wring your hands

I'll bring the popcorn

A snowflake fell
Into my mitten
Looked at me
Regretful
While the other snowflakes
Landed on a copper statue
Gathered there

Central park
I sucked on tic tacs
From my pocket
Breathed out icy air
And swore *i'll save you*
Tried to keep the star
From melting

On the night you disappeared

Jordan Claire McCraw

The little girl
Who suffers
And survives
Begets a woman

She'll go through it

Hiding in a xl
Teen boy's hoodie

Picking through fluorescent
Christmas candy

Listening to britney
In my headphones

Looking at cheap makeup
And fake leather

No one come the fuck near
Me today, please

Mom in target

Jordan Claire McCraw

I try not to
Remember you

The times i can't resist
I hold my heart back
From the open gate
She bucks and pulls
I grit my teeth
I watch you
Check you're nothing
That you're no one

Making sure

Then kick the gate shut with my boot and
Give the girl my full attention

Easy, love

The beauty contest
Turned me down

I guess it triggered
Me because

I only wanted
You, and your approval

Motherless

Will my whole life
Be forgotten

You gave me life
And forgot me

Confirmation bias

I want a sloppy paradise
Mixed drinks in sticky bars

I want kisses behind portaloos
While smelling of your sun cream

I want all-inclusive bus tours
Just a bloody getaway

Brits after brexit

Jordan Claire McCraw

This was a buffet
These people share me

You took some of everything
And went for seconds

Help yourself

Once upon a time
I had no god

But lived in fear of judgement

Then i should have died
But she revived me

Now i'm naked and don't care

I'm meant to be here

You know that scene
In the matrix

When they run in dodging bullets

Every time you take a breath
To speak
I think about it

I need backup

Jordan Claire McCraw

If i fucked you
In doc martens
Then i kicked you in the face
Would you be mad

My new aesthetic

I've come back
I announced
But no one came
Except for you

You snapped your fingers, *meet you there*

You drove all day
You came for jordan
With her glasses
And split ends

You cooed, *let's buy you clothes that fit*

Now when i come
They all find time
I'm cool to know
I'm hot to trot

They think i'm just so beautiful

But i remember

Jordan Claire McCraw

When the world
Blew up in flames

I pulled the rug out
From beneath me

Beat the fire
Til it smouldered

Tied that rug
Around my neck

And now you notice
Don't you, boy

This fucking cape

I want to kiss the man
Who smells of cigarettes
Because i make him nervous

Don't the other girls wear bras
You helpless creature

Second-hand smoke

Jordan Claire McCraw

Some blowhard
Made me laugh
I snorted coffee
Pushed my bangs back
From my eyes

Good fucking banter

I thought that i was
Realised

I thought i knew myself

I said *i do* and made a baby

I had finished growing

And then one day, god came along
And handed me a brick

Said *carry this*

Another chapter

It's only now
That i'm a mother

And i'm making decent choices
For my son

That i can see
How i was wired
By her choices
And i've lived them

Trojan horse

If
I
Tell
You
I
Want
To
Kiss
Your
Eyes
When
You're
Sleeping
Will
You
Think
I
Care
Too
Much

Nervous sext-er

Jordan Claire McCraw

There are things
I want to write
But then my husband
Is my sounding board

Don't hurt him

I want
To narcissus
The shit out of life

I want
To put make-up on
Just for myself

Please help
Me forget
That i'm lonely

My texts left on read

Jordan Claire McCraw

Is there a type of prostitution
Where we kiss men's adam's apples
While they're making funny jokes

Then they buy us better jeans

I'd break the law

I stepped into the shower
Just a tired mom
And felt you on my skin

You flooded back

So the world would know his goodness

I climbed mountains
And carved stories
On stone tablets

Golden calf

What does it look like
When a man first falls in love

I'm not sure that i know

He always loved me, true
But never stood still in the rain

His feet are dry

Jordan Claire McCraw

You ask for nudes
But then

My breasts

I fed them to my child

Both arms snapped beneath his weight

Venus de milo

I was just a child
When he married me

What would it be like now
To get engaged
And flash a ring
As my own person

Would i sparkle

Jordan Claire McCraw

I want to put on heels
And fix my makeup in the bathroom

Tell the other girls you're busy

Fucking had it

I knew myself
And mapped good choices
With sound information

But now i see new colors
And they've wrecked the fucking landscape

Wisdom sucks

Jordan Claire McCraw

She shuts the whole damn system down
Her mind goes blank
She knows the drill

She packs her sticks
She packs her stones

Another liar

Say my smile
Has you dazzled
Scrunch your nose
Into my cheek

Some simple things

Jordan Claire McCraw

Even in
My own damn memoir
I am scared

That you will leave

That all of you will hate me

Borrowed time

I'm strong enough to end this

I'm the stopgap

I'll stop running

I will stay, declare my space

And when my insecure foundation

Breaks away

When levees shatter

And the ocean overtakes me

I will grieve

But i will know

That all my ancestors are watching

I was never meant to last

Are you real

Yes

Are you real

Yes

Are you still real

Yes

Making friends

When a man tells me
He wants me
For my body
I light up

I've been living at the gym

Then i panic
If he wants me
For my body
He won't want me for my soul

Pretentious ass

Jordan Claire McCraw

I'd like you
To knock on my door
Holding daisies

I'll grant us
The one awkward moment
To search for a vase
Before making out

You and your gestures

I did not know the meaning of my sex
Until i watched my baby's head
Rupture tissue after tissue
As he panicked to the surface
And i threw my soul away
Without a thought
So he could breathe

Just cut him out

And so he lived

But they had cored me like an apple

This collection is for all the women who have done everything "right" but who still end up in a gutter - who have an empowered sense of humor about it all, but who are also pissed off and unfulfilled. No more lies. No more pretending. Whether we have lost our self-concept to our own broken childhoods, to motherhood, to careers, to marriages, to the wrong lovers - it is time for women to champion one another's truths, to embrace our worth and to dispel the toxic expectations of perfection that we have placed on ourselves.

Borne out of my postpartum depression journey (and subsequent nervous breakdown) and sexual awakening in my thirties, my poems explore my most honest experiences of relationships, loss, healing and self-worth. This collection of poetry follows that trajectory of self-exploration through relationships which have broken down and brought me closer to my own truths, prior to and in the aftermath of hospitalization. Interspersed throughout are also poems which focus specifically on my bicultural heritage, immigration and motherhood; these themes highlight the complexity of and contrasts within every modern-day woman's quest for personal identity.

About the book

Jordan Claire McCraw is a writer and actress who was raised outside of Washington, D.C. Jordan was a 2008 graduate of the Gemstone Honors Program at the University of Maryland, receiving bachelor's degrees in Theatre Performance and English (Creative Writing for Poetry).

One week after graduating, Jordan moved to the UK to live with her now-husband, whom she had met while volunteering in West Africa. Jordan worked as a high school teacher of English and Drama in rural England until 2015, when the birth of her son and her subsequent struggle with postpartum depression inspired her to leave the workforce and return to her love of acting, becoming a voiceover actress for clients in London such as Mattel. Jordan is now a television, film and commercial actress based out of New York City. Jordan reached the Top 16 in the 2019 Maxim Cover Girl Competition as a women's mental health advocate, and she is a proud audiobook narrator for HarperCollins and the Library of Congress.

About the author

CPSIA information can be obtained
at www.ICGtesting.com
Printed in the USA
BVHW091602011120
592248BV00003B/100

9 781735 335605